KT-382-684

nutella®
MUG CAKES & MORE
quick and easy cakes, cookies and sweet treats

Keda Black
Photography by Frédéric Lucano

hardie grant books

CONTENTS

COCONUT MUG CAKE WITH NUTELLA®

PREPARATION TIME 3 MINUTES – COOKING TIME 1 MINUTE

SERVES 1

50 g (2 oz/scant ½ cup)
  plain (all-purpose) flour

4 tablespoons
  coconut milk

2 tablespoons caster
  (superfine) sugar

1 tablespoon NUTELLA®

2 teaspoons cocoa
  powder

¼ teaspoon baking
  powder

1 teaspoon desiccated
  coconut, for sprinkling

1. Using a fork, mix all the ingredients apart from the desiccated coconut together in a mug until smooth.
2. Place the mug in the microwave for 1 minute (800 watts) until the cake feels dry on top.
3. Sprinkle with the desiccated coconut and serve.

COLD CHOCOLATE DRINK WITH NUTELLA®

PREPARATION TIME 5 MINUTES

SERVES 2

2 tablespoons cocoa powder, plus extra for sprinkling

500 ml (17 fl oz/ 2 cups) milk

2 tablespoons NUTELLA®

100 ml (3½ fl oz/scant ½ cup) whipping cream

1. In a small bowl, add the cocoa powder with a dash of milk, and mix until it forms a paste.
2. Add the NUTELLA® and mix well.
3. Gradually add the remaining milk to the paste, whisking until there are no lumps.
4. Chill in the fridge.
5. Whip the cream until thick.
6. Serve the chocolate drink nice and cold, topped with the whipped cream and a sprinkle of cocoa powder.

BANANA VERSION
Blend a banana with the milk, cocoa and NUTELLA®.

MILKSHAKE VERSION
Blend the milk with 2 scoops of ice cream and the NUTELLA®.

RASPBERRY AND MARSHMALLOW MUG CAKE WITH **NUTELLA**®

PREPARATION TIME 3 MINUTES – COOKING TIME 2 MINUTES

SERVES 1

50 g (2 oz/scant ½ cup)
 plain (all-purpose) flour

2 teaspoons
 cocoa powder

3 tablespoons caster
 (superfine) sugar

¼ teaspoon
 baking powder

3 tablespoons milk

2½ tablespoons plain
 Greek yoghurt

1 tablespoon NUTELLA®

1 tablespoon crushed
 raspberries, plus extra
 for the topping

5 mini marshmallows,
 plus extra for sprinkling

1. Combine the flour, cocoa powder, sugar and baking powder in a mug.
2. Add the remaining ingredients and stir well to combine.
3. Cook in the microwave for 2 minutes (800 watts) or until a toothpick inserted into the centre of the cake comes out clean.
4. Allow to cool for 1 minute, then scatter the raspberries and mini marshmallows on top to serve.

CHOCOLATE ORANGE MUG CAKE WITH **NUTELLA**® DRIZZLE

PREPARATION TIME 5 MINUTES – COOKING TIME 2 MINUTES EACH

SERVES 2

45 g (1½ oz/scant ¼ cup)
  soft butter

110 g (4 oz/½ cup) caster
  (superfine) sugar

½ teaspoon orange
  extract

2 tablespoons
  orange juice

1 egg

150 g (5 oz/1¼ cups)
  self-raising flour

35 g (1¼ oz/¼ cup)
  cocoa powder

For the drizzle:

2 tablespoons NUTELLA®

30 g (1 oz/scant ¼ cup)
  milk chocolate chips

60 g (2 oz/scant
  ½ cup) icing
  (confectioners') sugar

50 ml (2 fl oz)
  orange juice

1. In a bowl, beat together the butter with the sugar until pale.
2. Stir in the orange extract, juice and egg. Add the flour and cocoa powder and mix until really smooth.
3. Ladle the mixture into 2 mugs – they should be ¾ full.
4. Microwave one at a time for 2 minutes (800 watts).
5. Make the drizzle. Add the NUTELLA®, icing sugar and orange juice to a saucepan and gently melt, over a medium heat. Drizzle over the mug cakes and serve immediately.

CLASSIC CHOCOLATE MOUSSE WITH NUTELLA®

PREPARATION TIME 20 MINUTES – CHILLING TIME 3 HOURS

SERVES 4

140 g (5 oz/scant
 1 cup) dark chocolate

60 g (2 oz/¼ cup)
 NUTELLA®

4 egg whites

a pinch of salt

250 ml (8½ fl oz/1 cup)
 whipping cream, plus
 extra for topping

chocolate sprinkles,
 to serve

1. Gently melt the chocolate in a bain-marie until just melted.
2. Remove from the heat. Add 2 tablespoons of just-boiled water and stir until slightly cooled.
3. Add the NUTELLA® and stir well to form a glossy mix.
4. Whisk the egg whites with the salt until stiff. Whip the cream until thick.
5. Fold the egg whites and cream gently into the NUTELLA® chocolate mix.
6. Divide the mixture between 4 small glasses or ramekins and chill in the fridge for at least 3 hours. Before serving, top with cream and sprinkles.

LIGHT CHOCOLATE MOUSSE WITH **NUTELLA**®

PREPARATION TIME 20 MINUTES – CHILLING TIME 3 HOURS

SERVES 4

**100 g (3½ oz/scant 1 cup)
 dark chocolate chips**

**60 g (2 oz/¼ cup)
 NUTELLA**®

2 egg whites

a pinch of salt

**250 g (9 oz/1 cup) plain
 or Greek yoghurt**

**decorative sprinkles,
 to serve**

1. Gently melt the chocolate chips in a bain-marie and allow to cool.
2. Soften the NUTELLA® by placing the jar in a saucepan of hot water. Remove 60 g (2 oz/¼ cup) and mix it with the melted chocolate. Set aside.
3. Whisk the egg whites with a pinch of salt until stiff.
4. Mix the yoghurt with the chocolate and NUTELLA® mix.
5. Add a tablespoon of the egg whites to the yoghurt mix to loosen, then fold in the rest of the egg whites.
6. Divide the mixture into 4 small glasses or ramekins and chill in the fridge for at least 3 hours.
7. Just before serving, top with decorative sprinkles.

SPICED BROWNIE MUG CAKE WITH NUTELLA®

PREPARATION TIME 5 MINUTES – COOKING TIME 1 MINUTE

SERVES 1

4 tablespoons plain
  (all-purpose) flour

3½ tablespoons milk

2 tablespoons caster
  (superfine) sugar

2 tablespoons ripe
  banana, mashed

1 tablespoon NUTELLA®

1 tablespoon milk
  chocolate chips, plus
  extra for sprinkling

½ teaspoon
  baking powder

⅛ teaspoon cinnamon

1. Combine all the ingredients in a mug, leaving a few chocolate chips for the topping.
2. Microwave for 1 minute (800 watts) or until a toothpick inserted into the centre comes out clean. Let it cool for 1 minute.
3. Sprinkle with chocolate chips and serve.

COFFEE MUG CAKE WITH NUTELLA®

PREPARATION TIME 5 MINUTES – COOKING TIME 1 MINUTE 30 SECONDS

SERVES 1

3 tablespoons plain
 (all-purpose) flour

3 tablespoons caster
 (superfine) sugar

1 tablespoon
 cocoa powder

1 teaspoon instant
 coffee powder

¼ teaspoon baking
 powder

1 tablespoon NUTELLA®

2 tablespoons milk

½ teaspoon vanilla
 extract

2 tablespoons
 vegetable oil, plus
 extra for greasing

1 egg

icing (confectioners')
 sugar or ice
 cream, to serve

1. In a bowl, add the flour, sugar, cocoa powder, coffee powder and baking powder, and stir.

2. In a small bowl, mix the NUTELLA® with the milk and vanilla extract, then add the oil and egg. Blend together using a fork, then fold this into the flour mixture.

3. Pour into a mug and microwave for 1 minute and 30 seconds (800 watts).

4. Finish with a dusting of icing sugar or serve with vanilla ice cream.

MINT CHOCOLATE MUG CAKE WITH **NUTELLA**®

PREPARATION TIME 3 MINUTES – COOKING TIME 1 MINUTE

SERVES 1

4 tablespoons plain
 (all-purpose) flour

3 tablespoons milk

1 tablespoon **NUTELLA**®

½ tablespoon
 vegetable oil

¼ teaspoon baking
 powder

¼ teaspoon
 peppermint extract

¼ teaspoon vanilla
 extract

whipped cream, to serve

chocolate sprinkles,
 to serve

1. Add all the ingredients into a mug and stir until well combined.
2. Microwave for 1 minute (800 watts) or until a toothpick inserted into the centre comes out clean.
3. Let it cool, then serve with whipped cream and chocolate sprinkles.

PEANUT BUTTER MUG CAKE WITH NUTELLA®

PREPARATION TIME 3 MINUTES – COOKING TIME 1 MINUTE 10 SECONDS

SERVES 1

3 tablespoons plain
  (all-purpose) flour

2 tablespoons caster
  (superfine) sugar

1½ tablespoons
  cocoa powder

¼ teaspoon
  baking powder

a pinch of sea salt

3 tablespoons milk

1½ tablespoons
  vegetable oil

1 tablespoon smooth
  peanut butter

1 tablespoon NUTELLA®

1. Mix together the flour, sugar, cocoa powder, baking powder and salt in a large mug. Pour in the milk, oil, peanut butter and NUTELLA®, and blend until smooth.

2. Place in the microwave for 1 minute and 10 seconds (800 watts). The cake will be risen as it comes out of the microwave and then it will sink as it cools. Don't worry, it will still taste delicious.

CAFÉ LIÉGEOIS WITH NUTELLA®

PREPARATION TIME 20 MINUTES

SERVES 2

2 teaspoons espresso instant powder

2 tablespoons cocoa powder

150 ml (5 fl oz/scant ¾ cup) whipping cream

2 tablespoons NUTELLA®

2–4 scoops chocolate or coffee ice cream

chocolate sprinkles, to serve

1. Make the espresso-chocolate mix by adding the espresso and cocoa powders to 40 ml (1½ fl oz) just-boiled water. Mix well and allow to cool completely, then chill.
2. Whip the cream until thick.
3. Add 1 tablespoon of NUTELLA® to the cold espresso chocolate and mix well.
4. Into each glass, put 1 or 2 scoops of ice cream, divide the coffee-chocolate mixture in half and pour over the top, add a ½ tablespoon of NUTELLA®, and finish with whipped cream and chocolate sprinkles.

VARIATIONS
Chocolate liégeois: use hot chocolate that has been chilled instead of the ice cream.

BANANA MUG CAKE WITH NUTELLA®

PREPARATION TIME 5 MINUTES – COOKING TIME 1 MINUTE 10 SECONDS

SERVES 1

1 tablespoon unsalted
  butter, melted

1 tablespoon NUTELLA®

1 egg, lightly beaten

1 tablespoon milk

1 ripe banana, mashed

3 tablespoons plain
  (all-purpose) flour

3 tablespoons soft
  light brown sugar

½ teaspoon baking
  powder

icing (confectioners')
  sugar, for dusting

1. Melt the butter and NUTELLA® in a mug for 10 seconds (800 watts) in the microwave.
2. Add the egg and milk and beat using a fork.
3. Add the banana and mix.
4. Now add the flour, brown sugar and baking powder and continue to mix with the fork until well combined.
5. Cook for 1 minute (800 watts) in the microwave. Just before serving, sprinkle with icing sugar. This is particularly good served with coffee ice cream.

GLUTEN-FREE MUG CAKE WITH NUTELLA®

PREPARATION TIME 5 MINUTES – COOKING TIME 1–1½ MINUTES EACH

SERVES 2

1 egg

**4 tablespoons peanut
flour (or any nut
flour of your choice)**

**4 teaspoons
cocoa powder**

**2 teaspoons caster
(superfine) sugar**

**½ teaspoon
baking powder**

4 teaspoons butter

4 tablespoons milk

2 tablespoons NUTELLA®

**icing (confectioners')
sugar, for dusting**

1. Beat the egg until combined in a small bowl.
2. Add the peanut flour, cocoa powder, sugar, baking powder, butter and milk. Mix together with a fork. Add the NUTELLA® and beat hard and fast, until thoroughly combined.
3. Pour into 2 mugs and microwave each cake one at a time for 1–1½ minutes (800 watts); the cakes should be well risen and spongey and dry on top.
4. Let cool, then dust with icing sugar and serve.

ALMOND MUG CAKE WITH NUTELLA®

PREPARATION TIME 5 MINUTES – COOKING TIME 1 MINUTE EACH

SERVES 2

8 tablespoons
  unsweetened
  almond milk

8 tablespoons plain
  (all-purpose) flour

4 tablespoons caster
  (superfine) sugar

2 tablespoons NUTELLA®

2 tablespoons
  almond butter

½ teaspoon baking
  powder

2 almonds, finely
  sliced, to serve

icing (confectioners')
  sugar, for dusting

1. Divide all the ingredients, except the flaked almonds and icing sugar, between 2 large mugs and stir until fully combined.
2. Cook each cake in the microwave one at a time for 1 minute (800 watts), or until a toothpick inserted into the centre comes out clean.
3. Let them cool for 1 minute, dust with icing sugar, top with the sliced almonds and serve.

LAVA MUG CAKE
WITH NUTELLA®

PREPARATION TIME 5 MINUTES – COOKING TIME 1 MINUTE 40 SECONDS EACH

SERVES 2

2 tablespoons butter

6 tablespoons milk chocolate chips

4 tablespoons caster (superfine) sugar

1 egg

2 tablespoons plain (all-purpose) flour

2 tablespoons NUTELLA®

1 teaspoon chopped pistachios, for sprinkling

1. Add 1 tablespoon of the butter and 3 tablespoons of chocolate chips into two large mugs. Microwave for 40 seconds (800 watts).
2. Stir 2 tablespoons of sugar into each mug.
3. In a bowl, beat the egg, then add half the beaten egg to each mug.
4. Mix in 1 tablespoon of flour to each mug. Add 1 tablespoon of NUTELLA® to the centre of each mug.
5. Cook each cake in the microwave one at a time for 1 minute (800 watts), until the tops of the cakes have turned opaque.
6. Let them cool for 1 minute and serve sprinkled with chopped pistachios.

STRAWBERRY MUG CAKE WITH NUTELLA®

PREPARATION TIME 10 MINUTES – COOKING TIME 2 MINUTES EACH

SERVES 2

1 large egg

2 tablespoons caster (superfine) sugar

2 tablespoons plain (all-purpose) flour

1 tablespoon NUTELLA®

1 tablespoon soft butter

1 teaspoon baking powder

1 teaspoon cinnamon

½ teaspoon vanilla extract

3 tablespoons chopped strawberries

For the glaze:

1 tablespoon butter

1 teaspoon NUTELLA®

60 g (2 oz/½ cup) icing (confectioners') sugar

¼ teaspoon vanilla extract

1 tablespoon double (heavy) cream

1. In a bowl, beat all the ingredients, except the strawberries, together until smooth. Fold in 2 tablespoons of strawberries. Pour half of the mixture into each mug, and cook in the microwave, one at a time, for 1 minute 30 seconds (800 watts). Let cool.
2. Make the glaze. Melt the butter in the microwave for about 30 seconds and combine with the NUTELLA®, icing sugar and vanilla extract.
3. Whisk through the cream. Pour the glaze over the mug cakes, top with the remaining strawberries, and serve.

BANANA AND **NUTELLA**® IN A GLASS

PREPARATION TIME 10 MINUTES

SERVES 4

3 cardamom pods

**50 g (2 oz/¼ cup)
 NUTELLA**®

**400 g (14 oz/
 1¾ cups) soft cheese**

12 mini palmier biscuits

2 bananas

1 lemon

1 orange

1. Blend or grind the seeds from the cardamom pods.
2. Set aside 1 tablespoon of NUTELLA® and mix the rest with the soft cheese and the cardamom.
3. Crush 8 mini palmier biscuits into crumbs, not too small.
4. Slice the bananas into rounds and sprinkle with a little lemon and orange juice (don't use up all the juice).
5. In 4 glass dishes, make layers in this order: banana, soft cheese with NUTELLA®, NUTELLA® on its own, crushed palmier biscuits. Decorate the tops with the remaining palmier biscuits, crushed into crumbs.

CREAMY CHOCOLATE DIP WITH NUTELLA®

PREPARATION TIME 10 MINUTES – COOKING TIME 10 MINUTES – CHILLING TIME 2 HOURS

SERVES 4

60 g (2 oz/scant
  ½ cup) milk chocolate

60 g (2 oz/¼ cup)
  NUTELLA®

600 ml (20 fl oz) milk

½ vanilla pod

4 egg yolks

1 tablespoon cornflour
  (cornstarch)

breadsticks (to serve)

1. Gently melt the chocolate in a bain-marie and allow to cool.
2. Soften the NUTELLA® by placing the jar in a saucepan of hot water. Remove 60 g (2 oz) and mix it with the melted chocolate. Set aside.
3. Heat the milk with the seeds from the vanilla pod until almost boiled.
4. Whisk the egg yolks with the cornflour. Pour the hot milk on top, whisking well until completely combined.
5. Return the saucepan to a low heat. Warm gently for 3–4 minutes, stirring constantly until the mixture thickens.
6. Remove from the heat and cool slightly. Mix the NUTELLA® with the warm chocolate cream and allow to cool or chill before serving with breadsticks for dipping.

MOCHA COFFEE WITH NUTELLA®

PREPARATION TIME 10 MINUTES – COOKING TIME 5 MINUTES

SERVES 2

50 ml (2 fl oz/
 1¼ cup) whipping
 cream (optional)

100 ml (3½ fl oz/
 scant ½ cup) milk

4 small shots of hot
 espresso coffee
 (or equivalent quantity
 made in an Italian
 stove-top coffee
 maker, or filter coffee
 made extra strong)

1½ tablespoons
 NUTELLA®

a little cinnamon
 or four-spice mix
 (pepper, cloves,
 nutmeg and ginger),
 for sprinkling

1. Whip the cream until thick (ideally, make a larger quantity and use the excess for another dessert).
2. Heat the milk.
3. Whisk the hot coffee with the NUTELLA® and add the milk. Gently reheat if necessary.
4. Pour the mocha into two mugs, top with whipped cream and sprinkle a little cinnamon or four-spice on top.

FUDGE WITH NUTELLA®

PREPARATION TIME 10 MINUTES – COOKING TIME 15–20 MINUTES – LEAVE TO REST FOR 2 HOURS

MAKES 15–20 PIECES

oil, for greasing

150 ml (5 fl oz/scant ¾ cup) milk

2 tablespoons butter

175 g (6 oz/¾ cup) caster (superfine) sugar

50 g (2 oz/¼ cup) NUTELLA®

1. Grease a 15 cm (6 in) square baking tray or plastic container with the oil.
2. Heat the milk, butter and sugar in a small saucepan over a medium heat, stirring until the butter has melted and the sugar dissolved. Bring to the boil, reduce the heat to low and simmer for 15–20 minutes, until the mixture is very thick.
3. Take the pan off the heat and stir in the NUTELLA®. Leave the mixture to cool for 5 minutes.
4. Use a whisk to beat the mixture vigorously. Pour into the prepared baking tray or plastic container and leave to set at room temperature for 2 hours before cutting into small squares.

MERINGUES WITH **NUTELLA**® CENTRE

PREPARATION TIME 20 MINUTES – COOKING TIME 4 HOURS

MAKES ABOUT
15 MERINGUES

5 egg whites

**a few drops of
coffee or hazelnut
essence (optional)**

**100 g (3½ oz/½ cup)
caster (superfine) sugar**

**100 g (3½ oz/¾ cup) icing
(confectioners') sugar**

**1 tablespoon
cocoa powder**

**50 g (2 oz/¼ cup)
NUTELLA®**

1. Preheat the oven to 90°C (190°F/Gas ¼). Line a baking sheet with baking paper.
2. Whisk the egg whites until stiff. If using, add the coffee or hazelnut essence, and sprinkle in both sugars. Whisk until you have a smooth, shiny mixture. Add the cocoa powder and mix.
3. With a piping bag or a spoon, shape 30 meringues onto the prepared baking sheet. Bake for at least 4 hours: the meringues should dry out rather than cook. Let cool completely.
4. Soften the NUTELLA® by putting the jar in a saucepan of hot water.
5. When the meringues have cooled, spread the bottoms with the softened NUTELLA® and sandwich pairs together.

STAR SHORTBREAD WITH NUTELLA®

PREPARATION TIME 20 MINUTES – COOKING TIME 12–15 MINUTES – LEAVE TO REST FOR 30 MINUTES

MAKES 8 BISCUITS

100 g (3½ oz/scant ½ cup) soft butter

200 g (7 oz) plain (all-purpose) flour, sifted

½ teaspoon baking powder

75 g (2½ oz/scant ¾ cup) icing (confectioners') sugar

a generous pinch of cinnamon or seeds of ½ vanilla pod

2 egg yolks

100 g (3½ oz/scant ½ cup) NUTELLA®

1. Mix together the butter, sifted flour, baking powder, icing sugar and cinnamon or vanilla seeds until you have a smooth mixture.
2. Add the egg yolks and bring together the mixture into a dough. Drizzle in a little water, if needed. Wrap the dough in cling film (plastic wrap) and let it rest in the fridge for at least 30 minutes.
3. Preheat the oven to 180°C (350°F/Gas 4). Line 2 baking sheets with baking paper.
4. Roll the dough fairly thin, about 3 mm (¼ in). Cut into rounds approximately 8–10 cm (3–4 in) in diameter using a pastry cutter or rim of a glass. Take half the cut circles and, using a star pastry cutter, cut shapes out of the dough.
5. Transfer the biscuits to the prepared trays and bake in the oven for 12–15 minutes. Cool the biscuits on a wire rack.
6. Spread the biscuits without holes with NUTELLA®, place the biscuits with holes on top and add a little more NUTELLA® to the holes. These biscuits will keep for several days in an airtight container.

CRUNCHY ALMOND TOFFEES WITH NUTELLA®

PREPARATION TIME 10 MINUTES – COOKING TIME 15 MINUTES – LEAVE TO REST FOR 2 HOURS

MAKES 15–20 TOFFEES

oil, for greasing

125 g (4 oz/½ cup) caster (superfine) sugar

40 ml (1½ fl oz) double (heavy) cream

50 g (2 oz/¼ cup) NUTELLA®

a pinch of salt

150 g (5 oz/1 cup) roughly chopped almonds

1. Grease a 15 cm (6 in) square baking tray or plastic container with oil.
2. Put the sugar in a saucepan with a splash of water. Set over a low heat and let the sugar melt, without stirring, until it comes to the boil and turns a light golden colour (about 180°C/350°F on a sugar thermometer).
3. Meanwhile, heat the cream in a saucepan, being careful not to let it boil.
4. When the caramel is ready, pour in the cream. Stir well, then add the NUTELLA® and the salt. Finally, stir through the almonds.
5. Pour the toffee mixture into the prepared tray or plastic container and leave to set for 2 hours at room temperature before cutting into squares.

TIRAMISU WITH NUTELLA®

PREPARATION TIME 25 MINUTES – LEAVE TO REST FOR 3 HOURS

SERVES 6

500 g (1 lb 2 oz)
  mascarpone

60 g (2 oz/¼ cup)
  of NUTELLA®

5 eggs

15 savoiardi sponge
  fingers (ladyfingers)

1 tablespoon caster
  (superfine) sugar

2 small shots of
  espresso coffee

1 tablespoon Kahlúa,
  Marsala, amaretto
  or a nut liqueur

cocoa powder,
  for sprinkling

1. Work the mascarpone with a spatula in a bowl to soften it. Put a third of it into another bowl and mix in the NUTELLA® (if it's cold, you may need to put the NUTELLA® jar in a bowl of hot water to soften it and make it easier to mix).

2. Separate the egg whites and yolks. Whisk 3 egg yolks with the sugar (you will not be using the other 2 yolks). Add the 'white' mascarpone.

3. Whisk the 5 egg whites until stiff. Very gently fold two thirds of the egg whites into the 'white' mascarpone, the other third into the NUTELLA® mascarpone.

4. Mix together the coffee and liqueur. Arrange the biscuits at the bottom of a dish (or in individual dishes), and pour over the coffee-liqueur mixture. Add a layer of white cream, a layer of NUTELLA® cream, then another layer of white cream and another layer of NUTELLA® cream. Allow to rest in the fridge for at least 3 hours.

5. Sprinkle with cocoa powder just before serving.

TRIFLE WITH NUTELLA®

PREPARATION TIME 30 MINUTES – COOKING TIME 15 MINUTES – CHILLING TIME 4 HOURS

SERVES 4

40 g (1½ oz/scant
 ⅓ cup) milk chocolate

60 g (2 oz/¼ cup)
 NUTELLA®

150 g (5 oz) sponge cake
 or other cake that can
 soak up liquid
 (Italian pandoro,
 madeleines, etc.)

2 pears in syrup,
 with the syrup

500 ml (17 fl oz/
 2 cups) milk

½ vanilla pod

5 egg yolks

1 teaspoon
 cornflour (optional)

250 ml (8½ fl oz/1 cup)
 whipping cream

morello cherries in syrup

1 banana

4 tablespoons toasted
 flaked almonds, for
 sprinkling

1. Gently melt the chocolate in a baine-marie and allow to cool slightly. Add the NUTELLA® and mix well.
2. In a separate bowl, soak the trifle sponges in the pear syrup.
3. Make a custard by warming the milk with the seeds from the vanilla pod. Whisk the egg yolks in a bowl with the cornflour (if using). Just before it simmers, pour the milk onto the eggs and whisk. Return to the saucepan and cook over a gentle heat until the mixture thickens, without letting it boil, for about 5 minutes. The cornflour helps prevent it from curdling: you can do without, but then you have to take more care, cook it more gently and therefore perhaps for longer.
4. Add the chocolate and NUTELLA® mix to the warm custard and leave to cool completely.
5. Whip the cream until thick.
6. Set out the trifles in small jars. Arrange a layer of pieces of cake soaked in pear syrup, then a few morello cherries, then a layer of pear and banana cut into small pieces, a layer of the NUTELLA® custard, and a layer of whipped cream. Refrigerate for at least 4 hours (or overnight).
7. Sprinkle with flaked almonds before serving.

WALNUT-BANANA MUFFINS WITH NUTELLA®

PREPARATION TIME 20 MINUTES – COOKING TIME 15 MINUTES

MAKES 6 LARGE
(OR 12 MINI) MUFFINS

50 g (2 oz/¼ cup) butter,
  plus extra for greasing

150 g (5 oz/1¼ cup) plain
  (all-purpose) flour

2 teaspoons baking
  powder

½ teaspoon salt

1 egg

125 ml (4 fl oz/
  ½ cup) milk

3 tablespoons caster
  (superfine) sugar

2 tablespoons
  cocoa powder

1 very ripe banana,
  mashed

50 g (2 oz/½ cup)
  chopped walnuts

75 g (2½ oz/¼ cup)
  NUTELLA®

1. Preheat the oven to 200°C (400°F/Gas 6). Grease a 6-hole muffin tin (or a 12-hole mini muffin tin), or line the holes with paper muffin cases.

2. Melt the butter in a small saucepan. Put the flour, baking powder and salt into a bowl and mix well with a whisk.

3. In a large measuring jug or a separate bowl, whisk together the melted butter, egg, milk, sugar and cocoa powder.

4. Pour the wet ingredients into the dry ingredients, and add the mashed banana and chopped walnuts. Lightly stir with a wooden spoon, taking care not to overdo it – some lumps should still remain.

5. Pour the batter into the muffin tin and bake in the oven for around 15 minutes, or until a skewer inserted into the centre of a muffin comes out clean.

6. Remove from the oven. Fill a piping bag with the NUTELLA® and pipe into the centre of the muffins.

TWO-TONE COOKIES WITH NUTELLA®

PREPARATION TIME 40 MINUTES – COOKING TIME 15 MINUTES

MAKES 8–10

95 g (3 oz/½ cup)
  soft butter

100 g (3½ oz/½ cup)
  caster (superfine) sugar

2 eggs

zest of ½ lemon,
  finely grated

110 ml (4 fl oz/
  ½ cup) buttermilk

250 g (9 oz/2 cups) plain
  (all-purpose) flour

1 teaspoon baking
  powder

a pinch of salt

250 g (9 oz/2 cups) icing
  (confectioners') sugar

60 ml (2 fl oz/¼ cup)
  double cream

60 g (2 oz/¼ cup)
  NUTELLA®

1. Preheat the oven to 180°C (350°F/Gas 4). Line a baking sheet with baking paper.
2. In a bowl, beat together 85 g (3 oz/scant ½ cup) of the soft butter and the sugar until the mixture is pale and light. Gradually add the eggs, lemon zest and buttermilk.
3. In another bowl, mix together the flour, baking powder and salt. Fold into the wet mixture.
4. Spoon the mixture onto the baking tray and bake in the oven for approximately 12 minutes. Allow to cool.
5. Mix 200 g (7 oz/1½ cups) of the icing sugar with about 2 tablespoons of boiling water to obtain a medium pouring consistency.
6. Use a pastry brush to spread the icing over half of each cookie.
7. Heat the cream and the remaining butter in a saucepan. Bring to the boil, take off the heat and cool slightly before stirring in the NUTELLA®, allowing it to melt. Add the remaining icing sugar and enough boiling water to make a spreadable paste. Use a brush to ice the remaining half of each cookie.
8. Transfer to a wire rack to set the icing.

RICE PUDDING WITH NUTELLA®

PREPARATION TIME 5 MINUTES – COOKING TIME 25 MINUTES

SERVES 4

500 ml (17 fl oz/
  2 cups) milk

½ vanilla pod
  or a pinch of cinnamon
  or 3 cardamom pods

50 g (2 oz/¼ cup)
  pudding rice

4 tablespoons
  crème fraîche
  or Greek yoghurt

60 g (2 oz/¼ cup)
  NUTELLA®

1. Heat the milk with either the vanilla pod split in half, the cardamom pods or the cinnamon.
2. Just before it comes to the boil, sprinkle in the rice. Stir it. Cook over a fairly low heat, stirring often, until the rice is soft and the pudding creamy (about 20 minutes). Take out the vanilla pod or cardamom pods.
3. Add the cream or yoghurt off the heat.
4. Pour the pudding into ramekins, then top each with 1 tablespoon of NUTELLA® when you are ready to serve. Can be served hot or cold.

MILLIONAIRE'S SHORTBREAD WITH **NUTELLA**®

PREPARATION TIME 25 MINUTES – COOKING TIME 40 MINUTES – LEAVE TO REST FOR 2 HOURS

MAKES ABOUT 9 PIECES

200 g (7 oz/¾ cup)
  soft butter

50 g (2 oz/¼ cup) caster
  (superfine) sugar

170 g (6 oz/scant
  1½ cups) plain
  (all-purpose) flour

50 g (2 oz/½ cup)
  fine semolina

a pinch of salt

For the topping:

200 g (7 oz/
  ⅔ cup) sweetened
  condensed milk

80 g (3 oz/scant
  ½ cup) butter

80 g (3 oz/scant ½ cup)
  caster (superfine) sugar

2 tablespoons light honey
  or agave syrup

135 g (4½ oz/
  ½ cup) NUTELLA®

30 g (1 oz/¼ cup)
  cocoa powder

1. Preheat the oven to 170°C (325°F). Grease a 20 cm (8 in) square baking tin with a little butter.
2. In a bowl, beat the soft butter and the sugar together.
3. In another bowl, combine the flour, semolina and salt. Add this to the butter and sugar, and mix to combine.
4. Put the mixture into the prepared baking tin, smoothing over the top. Bake in the oven for around 35 minutes. Allow to cool in the tin.
5. Make the topping. Put the condensed milk, butter, sugar and honey or agave syrup into a small saucepan. Set over a low heat to allow the butter to melt. Simmer gently, stirring frequently, for 7–8 minutes until thickened.
6. Pour the mixture over the shortbread to make a layer of caramel. Allow to harden (this takes around 1 hour).
7. Soften the NUTELLA® by putting the jar in a saucepan of hot water. Put the softened NUTELLA® in a bowl and mix with the cocoa powder. Add 40 ml (1½ fl oz/½ cup) of just-boiled water and combine until you have a glossy mix. Spread the mixture over the caramel and allow to set for at least 1 hour in the fridge.
8. Cut the shortbread into squares, in the baking tray.

MADELEINES TOPPED WITH NUTELLA®

PREPARATION TIME 20 MINUTES – COOKING TIME 12–15 MINUTES

MAKES 10 MADELEINES

2 eggs

50 g (2 oz/¼ cup) caster (superfine) sugar

150 g (5 oz/1¼ cups) plain (all-purpose) flour

a pinch of salt

100 g (3½ oz/½ cup) very soft unsalted butter

2 tablespoons milk

90 g (3 oz/scant ½ cup) NUTELLA®

1. Preheat the oven to 190°C (375°F/Gas 5) and grease a madeleine tray.
2. Whisk together the eggs and sugar until they are very pale and fluffy. Gently fold in the flour and salt, then add the butter and milk. Mix well.
3. Drop spoonfuls of the mixture into the madeleine wells without filling them to the top. Bake in the oven for 12–15 minutes, until golden (keep an eye on them so they don't burn as the baking time will depend on your oven). Allow to cool.
4. Soften the NUTELLA® by putting the jar in a saucepan of hot water.
5. Once the madeleines have cooled, carefully turn out of the mould, and use a pastry brush to lightly coat the base of each with NUTELLA®. Place the madeleines upside down on a dish and put in the fridge to set more quickly. Serve straight away or keep in an airtight container.

CREAM HORNS WITH NUTELLA®

PREPARATION TIME 30 MINUTES – COOKING TIME 12–15 MINUTES – LEAVE TO REST FOR 30 MINUTES

MAKES 8–10
CREAM HORNS

**2 tablespoons butter,
 for greasing**

**300 g (10½ oz) good-
 quality butter puff pastry**

1 egg, for glazing

**75 g (2½ oz/¼ cup)
 NUTELLA®**

**250 g (9 oz/1 cup)
 mascarpone**

1. Preheat the oven to 225°C (430°FGas 7). Grease some metal pastry cones.
2. Roll out the pastry into a thin rectangle approximately 35 cm (14 in) square. Cut the pastry into 3 cm (1¼ in) wide strips. Roll a strip of pastry around each cone, overlapping as you go. If necessary, use two strips for each cone. Glaze with the beaten egg.
3. Place the horns on a baking tray lined with baking paper then bake in the oven for 12–15 minutes. If you don't have enough cones to do them all at once, do the whole operation again, greasing the cones again before each bake.
4. Remove the cones and allow the horns to cool at room temperature.
5. Warm the NUTELLA® by putting the jar in a saucepan of hot water (don't let it get hot, as that might make the mascarpone curdle). Mix the NUTELLA® with the mascarpone.
6. Using a piping bag, fill the horns with the mixture and serve straight away.

WHITE CHOCOLATE MADELEINES WITH NUTELLA®

PREPARATION TIME 15 MINUTES – COOKING TIME 10–12 MINUTES

MAKES 30 MINI
MADELEINES

**100 g (3½ oz/⅓ cup)
very soft unsalted butter**

2 eggs

**50 g (2 oz/¼ cup) caster
(superfine) sugar**

**150 g (5 oz/1¼ cups)
plain (all-purpose) flour**

a pinch of salt

2 tablespoons milk

**80 g (3 oz/½ cup)
white chocolate, cut
into tiny squares**

**75 g (2½ oz/¼ cup)
NUTELLA®**

1. Preheat the oven to 190°C (375°F/Gas 5). Butter some mini madeleine baking tins.
2. Whisk the eggs and sugar together until they whiten, then gently fold in the flour and salt. Add the butter and milk. Mix well.
3. Put spoonfuls of batter into the tins without filling them completely. Push a small square of white chocolate into the top.
4. Put in the oven for 10–12 minutes, keeping an eye on the cooking (the baking time will depend on your oven).
5. Immediately after taking them out of the oven, pipe a little NUTELLA® into the middle of the madeleines using a piping bag or syringe.

PIZZA WITH NUTELLA®

PREPARATION TIME 30 MINUTES – LEAVE TO REST FOR 2 HOURS – COOKING TIME 10 MINUTES

MAKES 2 SMALL PIZZAS/
SERVES 4

**300 g (10½ oz/2½ cups)
strong bread flour**

1 teaspoon salt

**1 teaspoon dried yeast
(or 10 g/½ oz fresh yeast
from your local bakery)**

**150 ml (5 fl oz/scant
¾ cup) lukewarm water**

**3 tablespoons olive
oil, plus extra for
oiling the bowl**

**2 tablespoons
fine semolina**

For the topping:

**60 g (2 oz/¼ cup)
NUTELLA®**

**125 g (4½ oz/½ cup)
Greek yoghurt**

1. Prepare the pizza dough. Put the flour in a large bowl (or the bowl of a food processor fitted with a kneading attachment). Add the salt and make a well in the middle. Put the yeast into a small bowl, add a little of the lukewarm water, leave for 5 minutes, then stir (if you are using fresh yeast, put the yeast and water straight into the flour). Pour the yeast into the well, add the oil and the remaining lukewarm water.
2. Mix and knead the dough for 8–10 minutes. Put the dough into an oiled bowl, cover with lightly oiled cling film (plastic wrap) and leave to rise for 2 hours.
3. Preheat the oven to its maximum temperature (250°C/500°F/ Gas 9) and put 2 baking sheets inside to heat up.
4. Divide the dough in 2 halves and roll each half out very thinly into a round on a floured work surface.
5. Sprinkle the hot baking sheets with semolina and put the pizza dough on top. Bake in the oven for 10 minutes.
6. Soften the NUTELLA® by putting the jar into a saucepan of hot water. Mix the yoghurt with half of the NUTELLA®.
7. Take the pizzas out of the oven and spread the remaining NUTELLA® over the top. Criss-cross with the NUTELLA® yoghurt mixture.

GATEAU LOUISE WITH NUTELLA®

PREPARATION TIME 35 MINUTES – COOKING TIME 35 MINUTES

SERVES 10

250 g (9 oz/1 cup)
  very soft butter, plus
  extra for greasing

200 g (7 oz/1 cup) caster
  (superfine) sugar

4 eggs, at room
  temperature

100 g (3½ oz/¾ cup)
  plain (all-purpose) flour

75 g (2½ oz/scant
  ¾ cup) ground
  hazelnuts (or almonds)

100 g (3½ oz/½ cup)
  dried apricots, finely
  chopped (optional)

75 g (2½ oz/¼ cup)
  NUTELLA®

200 g (7 oz/1 cup)
  marzipan

150 g (5½ oz/1¼ cups)
  icing (confectioners')
  sugar, plus extra
  for dusting

1. Preheat the oven to 180°C (350°F/Gas 4). Butter and line the base of a 20 cm (8 in) square cake tin with baking paper.
2. Beat the butter and sugar together until the mixture is light, very pale and fluffy. Mix in the eggs, one at a time, then gently fold in the flour, ground hazelnuts and the apricots if using. Pour this mixture into the prepared tin and bake in the oven for approximately 35 minutes, or until the tip of a knife inserted into the centre comes out clean.
3. Leave the gateau to cool for 10 minutes then turn out. Leave to cool for approximately 20 minutes, then spread the top with the NUTELLA® – reserving about 3 tablespoons for decoration.
4. Roll out the marzipan very thin on a work surface dusted with icing sugar – it should be a little larger than the gateau. Lay this marzipan on the cake: it should be the size of the top of the cake with a border of about 5 mm (¼ in).
5. In a bowl, mix the icing sugar with just enough water to make a very slightly runny icing. Pour over the cake, spreading with a spatula. Allow to set for 15–20 minutes at room temperature.
6. Fill a piping bag with the remaining NUTELLA® and decorate the gateau as you wish. This is a fairly rich gateau to be served in small portions.

LEGAL DISCLAIMER

This book and the recipes contained herein are the Author's own original creative work and they are in no way sponsored, endorsed by or associated with Ferrero Group. Nutella® is a registered trademark of Ferrero. The recipes in this book are intended for domestic use only. The realization of such recipes gives no permission to use the Nutella® trademark.

NUTELLA® MUG CAKES AND MORE

First published in 2012 by Hachette (Marabout)

This English hardback edition published in 2016 by Hardie Grant Books

Hardie Grant Books (UK)
52–54 Southwark Street
London SE1 1UN
hardiegrant.co.uk

Hardie Grant Books (Australia)
Ground Floor, Building 1
658 Church Street
Melbourne, VIC 3121
hardiegrant.com.au

The moral rights of Keda Black to be identified as the author of this work have been asserted by her in accordance with the Copyright, Designs and Patents Act 1988.

Text © Keda Black
Photography © Frédéric Lucano
Text on pages 4, 8, 10, 14, 16, 17, 18, 22, 24, 26, 28 & 30 © Fern Green
Photography on pages 5, 9, 11, 15, 16, 17, 19, 23, 25, 27, 29 & 31 © Danielle Wood

All rights reserved. No part of this publication may be reproduced, stored in a retrieval system or transmitted in any form by any means, electronic, electrostatic, magnetic tape, mechanical, photocopying, recording or otherwise, without the prior written permission of the Publisher.

British Library Cataloguing-in-Publication Data. A catalogue record for this book is available from the British Library.

ISBN: 978-1-78488-076-7

Photograph on page 5 and cover: Richard Boutin
Design: Sonia Lucano
Layout: Frédéric Voisin
Editing: Véronique Dussidour

For the English hardback edition:
Publisher: Kate Pollard
Senior Editor: Kajal Mistry
Editorial Assistant: Hannah Roberts
Additional recipes: Fern Green
Additional photography: Danielle Wood
Recipe tester: Juliet Sear
Colour Reproduction by p2d

Printed and bound in China by 1010

10 9 8 7 6 5 4 3